STEP-BY-STEP CRAFTS

CANDLE MAKING

CHERYL OWEN

NEW HOLLAND

This edition first published in the UK in 2003 by
New Holland Publishers (UK) Ltd
London · Cape Town · Sydney · Auckland
www.newhollandpublishers.com

Garfield House, 86-88 Edgware Road
London W2 2EA
United Kingdom

80 McKenzie Street
Cape Town 8001
South Africa

Level 1, Unit 4, 14 Aquatic Drive
Frenchs Forest, NSW 2086
Australia

218 Lake Road
Northcote, Auckland
New Zealand

ISBN 1 85974 876 7

Editor: Kate Latham
Photographer: John Freeman

Editorial Direction: Rosemary Wilkinson
Project Editor: Clare Johnson

10 9 8 7 6 5 4 3 2 1

Reproduction by
Pica Colour Separation, Singapore
Printed and bound in Malaysia by
Times Offset (M) Sdn. Bhd.

Important
The author and publishers have made every effort to ensure that all instructions given in this book are safe and accurate. They cannot accept liability for any resulting injury or loss or damage to either property or person, whether direct or consequential and howsoever arising.

Acknowledgements

The author and publishers would like to thank Candle Makers Supplies and The Pier for their help in providing props for photography.

STEP-BY-STEP CRAFTS

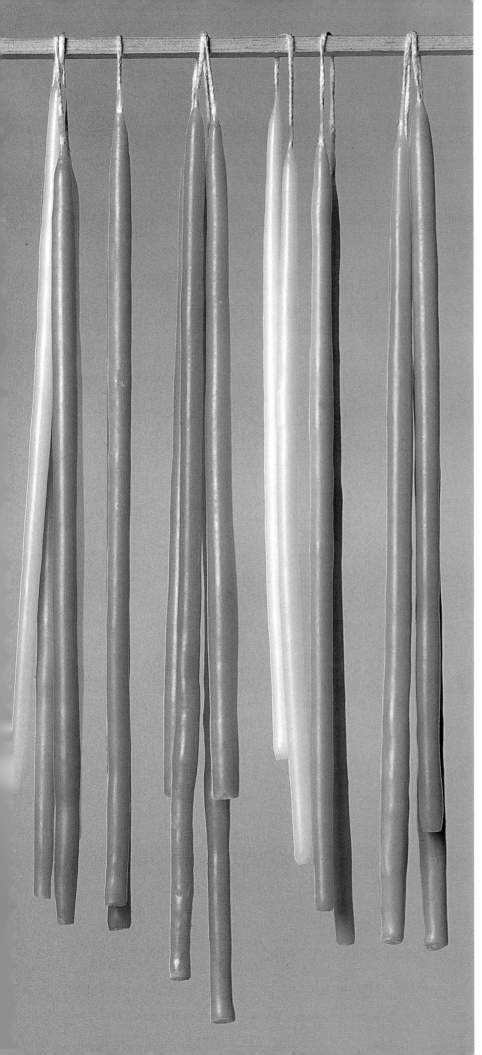

Contents

Introduction

Although, thanks to electricity, candles are no longer a necessity in our lives, they are still a pleasure. The warm flicker of candlelight can quickly alter the mood and atmosphere of a room, often creating a tranquil, ambient scene that electric light just cannot match.

Candles are an important part of many cultural and religious festivals and have been burnt in various forms for centuries. The Romans and ancient Egyptians made candles from flax coated with pitch and wax, and before the nineteenth century most candles were made from a substance called tallow, obtained from beef fat. Tallow candles were very smoky and, understandably, had an unpleasant smell.

Stearin was separated from tallow in the nineteenth century, and was used to harden other fats. Candles that contained stearin would burn longer than previously and had no nasty odour. The extraction of paraffin wax from coal and peat improved the quality of candles even further. Paraffin wax and stearin are still the main components of modern candle making, and the techniques used to create candles today are the same as have been used for many years. However, the increased range of wax dyes, perfumes and other additives that are now available make candle making a very exciting and contemporary craft.

Sales of candles have increased dramatically in the last few years, showing that they have become part of our lives again, not through necessity this time, but because of the magical atmosphere they create. In our increasingly stressful lives, the soothing quality of candlelight has a relaxing effect that many enjoy.

This book introduces beginners and more experienced candle makers to the range of materials and techniques that can be used to create unique candles. Familiarize yourself with the "Getting Started" section and you will have the grounding you need to tackle the projects that follow, or even make your own designs. The projects cover many aspects of this craft, including making your own moulds, layering wax stripes, embedding small objects, and making garden flares and delicate floating flowers. There are also examples of decorative effects that can be applied to finished candles, such as stencilling, freehand painting and applying appliqué wax and metal leaf.

Candle making is most definitely enhanced by the exciting possibilities of experimentation. So, be bold and try out different effects – some of the most wonderful creations can happen by accident. You will be amazed at the very professional finish that can be achieved.

Despite its fragile beauty, candlelight can, of course, be highly dangerous. So please remember to never leave lighted candles unattended or in a draught, to always stand candles securely in holders and to place them out of the reach of young children and animals.

Cheryl Owen

Getting Started

Candle making is not an exact science and that is what makes it so exciting and intriguing. Have fun experimenting with the techniques, and remember that unsuccessful candles can be melted and the wax used again. This section outlines the equipment and materials needed for candle making, and the basic techniques are clearly explained to help you create the projects that follow.

If you are making candles at home, the kitchen is probably the best place to work since it houses a source of heat and water. Protect your work surface with plenty of newspaper to catch the unavoidable spills of wax, and remember to gather together all the equipment and materials you will need before you embark on a project, so that you do not have to leave heating wax unattended while you look for them.

GENERAL EQUIPMENT

Much of the equipment needed to make candles can be found among your basic kitchen and desk equipment. Other, specialist items are available from candle-making suppliers or craft shops.

SAFETY FIRST

Candle making is a safe pastime if you follow a few "common sense" rules:

- Always heat wax in a double boiler or a metal bowl or small saucepan over a saucepan of water. Wax heating directly in a saucepan can quickly overheat and ignite. For the same reason, do not allow the water to boil dry.

- Monitor the temperature of the molten wax with a thermometer. If paraffin wax reaches a temperature higher than 100°C (212°F) it will begin to smoke and is in danger of igniting.

- Never leave heating wax unattended.

- Keep children and animals away when working with hot wax.

- If wax does ignite, do not use water to put out the flames. Switch off the heat source, then smother the flames with a saucepan lid, damp towels or a fire blanket.

Double boiler

Wax can easily overheat and ignite when molten, so, for safety, melt wax in a double boiler, with water in the lower pan and wax in the upper pan. Alternatively, heat the wax in a small saucepan resting on a trivet that sits in a larger saucepan of water.

Dipping can

Long, thin candles are made by dipping lengths of wick into wax housed in a dipping can – a tall, cylindrical, metal vessel. You can also try improvizing with a large metal food can or a metal bucket, but these will need to be filled with more wax than the thin dipping can to reach the required height.

Thermometer

Molten wax needs to be poured at specific temperatures to achieve the right effect. Therefore, an essential piece of equipment is a thermometer. This can either be a wax thermometer, available from candle-making suppliers, or a sugar thermometer.

Weighing scales

Use kitchen scales to weigh wax and stearin.

Cocktail stick

Use a cocktail stick, or a kitchen skewer, to support the wick in the mould, keeping it vertical and central while you pour in the wax. Simply tie one end of the wick around the stick and rest it across the open shoulder of the mould.

Craft knife

Use a craft knife to cut and score lines in card when making moulds. It can also be used to cut soft wax.

Knife

Keep a small knife close at hand. Use it to cut through soft wax and to shave off slithers of dye discs.

Pouring jug

This is a useful but not vital piece of candle-making equipment. If you are nervous of pouring hot wax from a saucepan into a mould, decant the wax into a metal jug with a spout that will give you more control.

Ruler

An ordinary stationery ruler is used to measure depths on a mould. You will also need to draw straight lines against a ruler when making your own moulds. Use a craft knife against a metal ruler to score or cut straight lines.

Scissors

Use scissors to trim the wicks of finished candles and to cut out paper templates.

Adhesive tapes

Use masking tape to mark measurements on moulds, to tape down templates or stencils and to paint straight lines. Strong waterproof tape should be used to seal moulds made from card.

Card

Thin card is a good material to use as a template when making your own moulds or decorative motifs. Thick card is used to construct homemade moulds.

Cutting mat

A cutting mat will protect your work surface whenever you use a craft knife, and it can be used again and again. Alternatively, you could try resting on a few layers of corrugated cardboard.

Greaseproof paper

Greaseproof paper can be dipped into coloured molten wax and left to dry to determine the shade of the finished candle. It is also useful for saving excess wax: simply pour the molten wax into a bowl lined with greaseproof paper and leave it to solidify.

Kitchen towel

Kitchen towel is indispensable for mopping up wax and cleaning equipment.

Oven gloves

Although the temperature the wax is poured at for the projects in this book is not hot enough to burn, you may find it comfortable to wear oven gloves while you work.

Weights

Most moulds filled with wax will float in a water bath, so place a heavy weight on top of the mould to keep it in place. Clean pebbles or old-fashioned kitchen weights work well.

WAX

Appliqué wax

This wax is used as decoration on formed candles. It is available as thin sheets that can be cut into shapes and pressed onto a candle without the need for extra glue. Appliqué wax can be bought in a wide range of colours, including metallics, and as precut motifs.

Beeswax

This fragrant wax is available in block form, or in a variety of colours in sheet form. The sheets can be moulded into rolled candles without being heated.

Crystal wax

Dip set candles in crystal wax melted at 71°C (165°F) to produce a frosted, crystal effect on the surface.

Dip and carve wax

This specially blended wax is more malleable than paraffin wax and so can be modelled by hand and will not splinter when carved.

Jelly wax

This wax really does feel like jelly. It has a high melting point – it is poured at 110°C (215°F) – and should be coloured very sparingly with powder dye (see page 11). Jelly wax does not set solid in the same way as paraffin wax, so can only be used to make container candles, usually in a glass vase that reveals its unique, bubbly finish.

Microcrystalline

There are two types of mycrocrystalline that are added to paraffin wax to alter its properties. Soft microcrystalline has a low melting point and can be added to paraffin wax – use 10-20% – to make it malleable and therefore suitable for modelling. Hard microcrystalline has a high melting point. Add just 1% to paraffin wax to make your candles slower burning.

Paraffin wax

Most candles are made from paraffin wax, which is a by-product of petrol. Paraffin wax

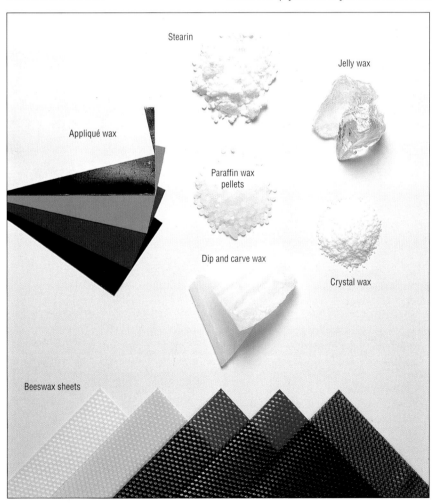

can be bought in pellet and slab form. The pellets are easier to weigh than the slabs, which need to be broken up with a chisel.

Stearin

Stearin is derived from palm nuts. Mixing stearin with paraffin wax causes the wax to contract, therefore making the candle easy to release from the mould. Stearin also makes the wax more opaque and enhances the dye colours used. Use 90% paraffin wax to 10% stearin. It is not necessary to use stearin when working with flexible moulds.

Wax glue

This very sticky wax is used to glue wax surfaces together and to glue embellishments to candles. Spread the wax glue with a knife.

Plaited wicks

This cotton wick is made from three plaited strands of smaller strands. It is the most commonly used type of wick and available in various thicknesses that suit the size of the candle being made. For example, a 2.5 cm (1 in) wick is designed to be used in a 2.5 cm (1 in) diameter candle: the wick itself is not 2.5 cm (1 in) in diameter. If you use a wick that is too small, the burning wax will not form a pool that reaches to the outside of the candle, but will burn in a small pool around the wick that the wax will drip into, drowning the flame. If the wick used is too large, it will produce a large flame and the candle will smoke. When making a cone, triangular or pyramid candle, choose a wick size about half the width of the candle base.

Pliers

A pair of pliers can be used to secure a wick in a wick sustainer and to pull a wick through a hole.

Wicking needle

This long needle has many uses. Use it to pierce holes in wax, to thread a wick through a hole in the wax or the mould and to support a wick in a large mould: tie the wick to the needle and rest it across the shoulder of the mould. A large darning needle can be used instead.

Wick sustainer

These metal discs, available in two sizes, have a hole in the centre and are used to hold the wick in container candles or some freestanding candles made without a mould.

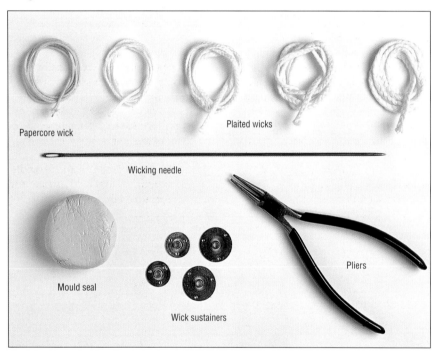

Papercore wick

Plaited wicks

Wicking needle

Mould seal

Wick sustainers

Pliers

MOULDS

Candle makers have a wide choice of moulds at their disposal. Ready-made candle moulds are made of plastic, metal, glass or latex, or you can make your own moulds using household containers, card or baking foil.

Baking foil

Baking foil can be folded into small, shallow square trays that wax is then poured into. When the wax cools and becomes rubbery it can be removed from the foil mould and cut into shapes.

Baking moulds

Use cookie cutters to cut shapes out of semi-set, rubbery wax. Chocolate mould shapes are especially good for making floating candles.

WICKS

Mould seal

Mould seal is a putty-like substance that is used to seal a wick in place and cover the wick hole in a mould so that wax cannot seep out and water cannot seep in. Mould seal is reusable.

Papercore wicks

Papercore wicks are suitable for use in container candles and are available in three sizes. Use a small wick in a candle with a diameter up to 5 cm (2 in). Use a medium wick in a candle with a diameter of 6.5 cm (2½ in). Use a large wick in a candle with a diameter of 7.5 cm (3 in) or more.

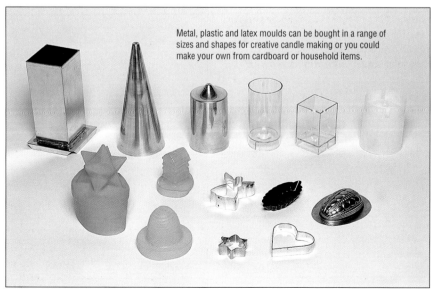

Metal, plastic and latex moulds can be bought in a range of sizes and shapes for creative candle making or you could make your own from cardboard or household items.

Baking tray

Wax can be poured into a clean baking tray then cut to shape when it has cooled and become rubbery.

Card moulds

You can make your own moulds from thick card or use waxed paper drink cartons.

Glass moulds

A heatproof glass oven dish can make a great candle mould. In order to release the candle, use a dish that is straight sided or that tapers to the base.

Latex moulds

These flexible moulds are designed for making intricately shaped candles, and the inside must be coated with a special mould release before pouring in the wax. A flexible mould needs to be securely supported over a bowl or jar while the wax is poured in and as it cools.

Metal moulds

Metal moulds are very hardwearing but quite expensive compared to plastic moulds.

Plastic moulds

Plastic moulds are the most versatile of all moulds. They can be found in a range of shapes and sizes, they are inexpensive, transparent, which means you can see what is happening inside, and they can be used many times.

CONTAINERS

When making a container candle, the initial choice of container is important. The container must be heatproof, but it should also suit the style of candle you are creating. For example, you would not want to hide the effects of a jelly candle in a china container, but if you are worried that

Making a foil tray

a finished candle might not look as it should, then a china container is the perfect choice to hide any mishaps.

Glass and ceramic containers

Make sure the container is heatproof. Gently heat a glass or ceramic container with some warm water before you pour hot wax in, to ensure that the container does not crack on contact with the wax.

Metal containers

Metal will become very hot when a candle is burning inside so always place metal container candles on a protected surface.

COLOUR AND PERFUME

Acrylic paint

Acrylic paint can be applied directly to a fully cooled candle to add some applied decoration.

Ceramic paint

To embellish a glass container, use ceramic paint to decorate the outside of the container before the candle is made. Use stripes or a basic stencil that will allow the candle to show through.

Dye discs

Dye discs are blocks of wax with concentrated pigments. You can either dissolve the dye in stearin or directly in wax if stearin is not being used. An indication of the quantities of dye needed to produce the basic colour is specified by the manufacturer, but the discs are easy to cut so you can add as much or as little as you like. For the projects in this book only small amounts of dye are needed. To test the true colour allow a sample of dyed wax to cool on some greaseproof paper. You can also mix dyes to produce your own shades.

Powder dye

These dyes are very strong and only a very small amount is needed to create the colour. Dissolve the powder completely in stearin, wax or jelly wax. Handle powder dye carefully as it is very messy.

Wax perfume

Only use perfumes that are specially formulated for use in candles. Be aware that some wax perfumes can affect the colour of a candle so use them sparingly, 6% of perfume to wax is a recommended amount. Add the perfume to the heated wax just before you make the candle. Perfume is more effective in a wide candle than a taper since it contains more molten wax to release the scent.

Powder dyes

Wax perfumes

Acrylic paint

Dye discs

Ceramic paint

PREPARING THE WAX

Weighing

The amounts of wax and stearin given in the "you will need" lists that accompany the projects tell you the quantities needed for a particular project, but they can also be referred to as a guide when making your own candles of a similar size. To be on the safe side, always melt more wax than you think you will need, especially when dying the wax since to mix a second batch in exactly the same shade could be extremely difficult. Excess wax can always be remelted and used again.

If you are making a candle in a reusable rigid mould, such as a commercial plastic mould or a heatproof glass oven dish, you will need to include stearin with the wax in order to easily release the candle from the mould when it has cooled. Use 10% stearin to 90% wax.

Melting the wax and stearin

To prevent the danger of wax igniting, it must be heated over water. Using a double boiler is the safest way to do this. Alternatively, heat the wax in a small saucepan resting on a trivet in a larger saucepan of water. It is often useful to have two double boilers in action at the same time when heating wax and stearin separately. If you only have one double boiler, use the double boiler to heat the stearin and two saucepans to heat the wax. Test the temperature of both with a wax or sugar thermometer.

Colouring wax

Small amounts of dye discs are usually added to the stearin before it is mixed with the wax. If you are not using stearin, add the dye directly to the molten wax in the same way.

A little dye goes a long way, so be cautious when adding it. You can shave off small pieces of the disc with a knife. Then stir the colour in with a spoon. Or, if you intend to use a large amount of the dye disc, crush the disc or a part of it with a spoon on greaseproof paper before stirring it into the stearin or wax.

Adding the wax to the stearin

When both the wax and stearin are molten, and the dye has dissolved in the stearin if colouring, pour the wax into the stearin and stir the ingredients together.

It is a good idea to test the colour since it will change as it cools. Drop a teaspoonful of coloured wax onto some greaseproof paper and allow it to cool, to reveal the finished shade (see page 12). Remember that you can mix different coloured dye discs to produce exactly the shade you want.

PRIMING THE WICK

Priming the wick for a paraffin candle

The wick needs to be primed with wax so that it is easy to light and will burn well.

Usually only the wick that protrudes from the candle needs to be primed, but it can be easier to prime a length of wick and cut off the amount you need once it has cooled. To prime the wick simply dip it into the molten wax for a few seconds to allow the wax to soak in. Remove the wick from the wax, let it cool, then straighten it between your fingers.

Priming the wick for a rolled beeswax candle

The wick in a rolled beeswax candle will not have been primed, so tear off a small piece of a beeswax sheet and simply wrap it around the exposed wick before lighting.

POSITIONING THE WICK

Positioning the wick in a plastic mould

First make sure the mould is clean. The wick should be at least 7.5 cm (3 in) longer than the height of the mould. From the inside of the mould, insert the primed wick through the hole at the base.

Rest a cocktail stick or wicking needle across the shoulder of the mould and tie the wick around it. This support will keep the wick centrally positioned.

Pull the wick taut through the hole at the base and secure it in place by pressing a piece of mould seal around the extending wick and the hole. This will stop wax seeping out and water seeping in. The base of the mould will become the top of the candle.

Fixing the wick in a sustainer

A wick in a container candle, and in some freestanding candles, is held in place with a wick sustainer. Poke the end of the primed wick into the hole in the sustainer. Use a pair of pliers to tighten the metal around the wick to anchor it in place.

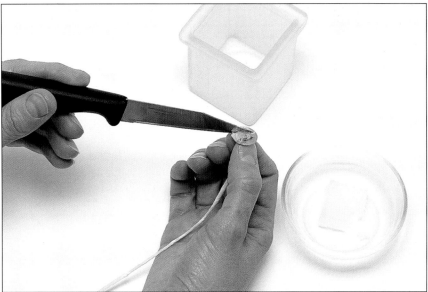

Fixing the wick in a container

Use a knife to spread wax glue on the underside of the sustainer. Position the sustainer in the centre of the base of the container and press down to fix it in place. If you do not have wax glue, use a small piece of mould seal instead. Tie the end of the wick around a cocktail stick or wicking needle and rest it across the top of the container.

Making a hole

Some candles, especially stacked candles and those shaped from thin slabs of semi-set wax formed in a baking tray, have the wick inserted after the wax has cooled. When the wax feels rubbery to the touch but is not completely set, use a wicking needle to pierce a hole through it. Make sure the hole is big enough for the primed wick. If necessary, the hole can be enlarged when the wax has cooled completely by heating the end of the needle in a flame and pushing it into the hole again.

Threading the wick

Because a primed wick is stiff, it is usually easy to thread it through holes in set wax. Use the point of a wicking needle if necessary to push the wick through a tight hole.

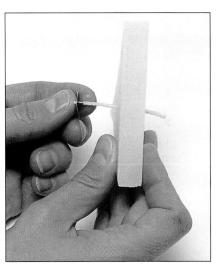

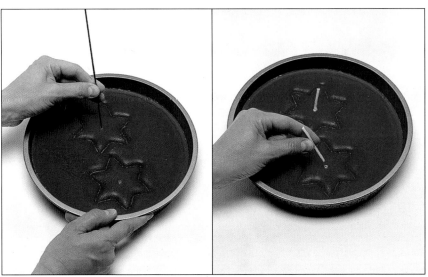

MAKING THE CANDLE

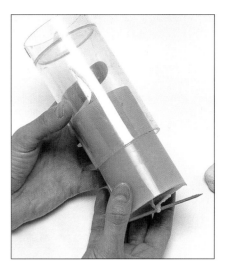

1. Carefully pour the molten wax into the mould at the temperature specified in the project. For paraffin wax candles the temperature should be 82°C (180°F). To make jelly candles and create the frosted effect the temperatures differ (see pages 60–63 and 88–91). Fill the mould to just below the wick support, or to a specific mark on the mould if you have made one. Keep the excess wax in the double boiler for topping up later. After about 1 minute, tap the side of the mould with a spoon or knife to release any trapped air.

2. Stand the mould in a deep bowl or bucket and place a weight on top of the mould to anchor it in position. Pour water into the bowl up to the level of the wax. Standing the mould in a water bath like this will cool the wax quite quickly.

3. Remove the mould after about 1 hour. A well will have formed around the wick. Prick the wax around the wick with a needle.

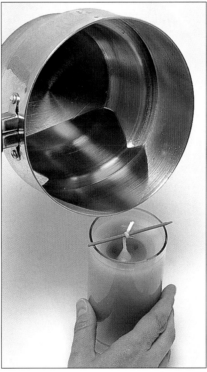

4. Reheat the wax to the same temperature as before and pour it into the well to just below the level of the previous pouring. The wax needs to be topped up or the candle may become distorted. Large candles may need topping up more than once. When you have topped up the candle for the last time, pour any excess molten wax into a bowl lined with greaseproof paper and leave to cool. You can remelt the wax at any time.

5. Return the mould to the water bath to cool completely. Remove the mould from the bath and peel off the mould seal. Slip the candle out of the mould and remove the cocktail stick. Cut off the wick under the candle as close as possible to the wax with a pair of scissors. Trim the wick at the top of the candle to 1.5 cm (⅝ in).

6. To flatten the base of the candle, gently heat a saucepan. Hold the candle in the pan for a few seconds to melt the base and flatten it.

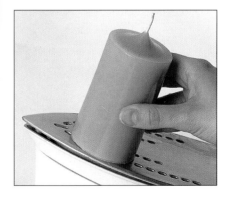

7. Another way to flatten the base is to hold the candle against a gently heated iron. Wipe the iron clean immediately after use with kitchen towels.

MAKING
YOUR OWN
SHAPES

1. Mark the intended depth of the wax with a strip of masking tape on the inside wall of a heatproof baking tray.

3. Use a ready made cookie cutter to stamp a shape into the wax. Alternatively, you can create your own shapes. Cut around a paper template with a knife or craft knife held upright. Pierce holes for a wick while the wax is still rubbery.

2. Pour the wax into the tray level with the tape. Allow the wax to cool for about 45 minutes and become rubbery but not completely set.

INSPIRATION

The projects described in this book may fit your needs perfectly, or you might want to adjust the designs in some way to suit your unique requirements. When designing your own candles, there are a few things to bear in mind.

First, consider the intended setting for the candles you propose to create, since this will influence their colour and dimensions. Candle holders that you already possess, such as lanterns and candelabras, will suggest the size of candles to make. Candles for a special meal should be quite low in height so that your guests can talk across the table without obstacle. A bowl of floating candles mingling with flower-heads makes a very attractive dinner table decoration.

It is possible to create a diverse range of candles to suit all lifestyles with just a little experimentation. Plain candles can easily be decorated to embellish the theme of their setting. For example, you could stencil or paint candles with Egyptian hieroglyphics, Aboriginal motifs or designs from nature such as leaves and flowers. Fine appliqué wax can be cut into intricate patterns and applied to candles, giving a very professional look to your creations.

Candles can instantly create an atmosphere and the use of scent will enhance this. The wide choice of wax perfumes available is bound to feature the fragrance you are looking for. On a practical level, anti-tobacco perfume will alleviate the smell of cigarettes and anti-midge perfume will keep irritating insects at bay when using candles in the garden. Other scents will evoke a mood of relaxation or rejuvenation and could be used in the bedroom or bathroom respectively. You could even recreate the feel of a sunny, summer garden in the depths of winter simply by lighting floral perfumed candles.

1
Beeswax Spirals

andles rolled from sheets of beeswax are very easy to
make, and since the wax does not need to be melted, it is
a great project for children to try: they can cut the beeswax
with a pair of scissors rather than a craft knife, for safety.
Beeswax smells delightful and the honeycomb patterned
sheets are simple to work with. One sheet of white and one of
natural beeswax will make one tall and one short candle.

You will need

1 sheet of white beeswax

1 sheet of natural beeswax

Cutting mat

Craft knife

Metal ruler

**50 cm (20 in) length of 4 cm
(1½ in) wick**

Scissors

1 On a cutting mat, use a craft knife
and a metal ruler to cut diagonally
across each beeswax sheet, from
5 cm (2 in) below the top of the top right-
hand corner to the bottom left-hand corner.
Set the smaller pieces aside.

2 Trim 1 cm (⅜ in) off the long
straight edge of the natural sheet.

3 Cut a 30 cm (12 in) length of unprimed wick and place it along the longest side edge of the white sheet, aligning one end of the wick with the long straight edge at the base of the sheet. Start to roll the wax around the wick until the wick is concealed.

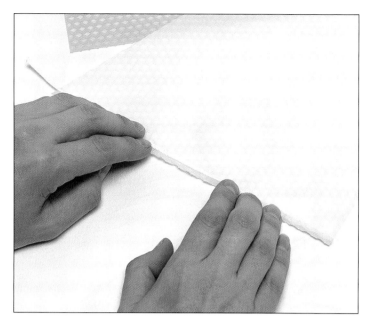

4 Lay the white, partially rolled sheet on top of the natural sheet, aligning the long, lower edges and the longest side edges. Roll the natural sheet around the concealed wick.

5 Continue rolling the candle, keeping the lower edges level.

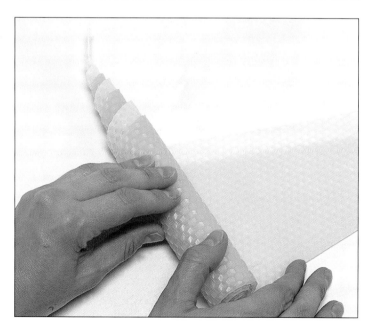

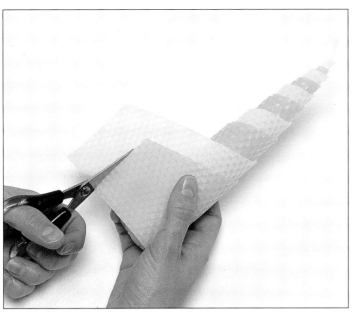

6 Before you reach the short edges, cut the white wax level with the natural wax using a pair of scissors. Press the short ends smoothly to the candle so that it does not unravel.

artist's tip

Sheets of beeswax are malleable at room temperature. If the sheets are cold and brittle, simply warm them with a hair-dryer.

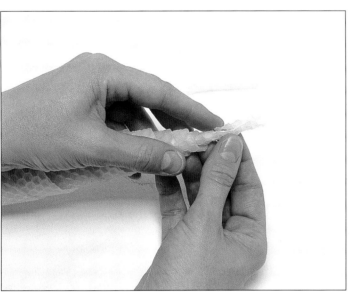

7 Tear off a small piece of the white discarded beeswax and wrap it around the wick to prime it. Cut the wick to 1.5 cm (⅝ in) before lighting it.

8 Use the leftover pieces of beeswax from Step 1 and a 20 cm (8 in) length of wick in the same way to make a shorter candle.

variation

To make a pair of traditional beeswax pillar candles, first cut a natural beeswax sheet in half lengthwise. Cut off a thin length of wax from one sheet to prime the wick, then roll each half sheet around a 15 cm (6 in) length of 2.5 cm (1 in) wick. Prime the wick with the slither of wax and cut it to 1.5 cm (⅝ in) before lighting.

2

Tiny Tapers

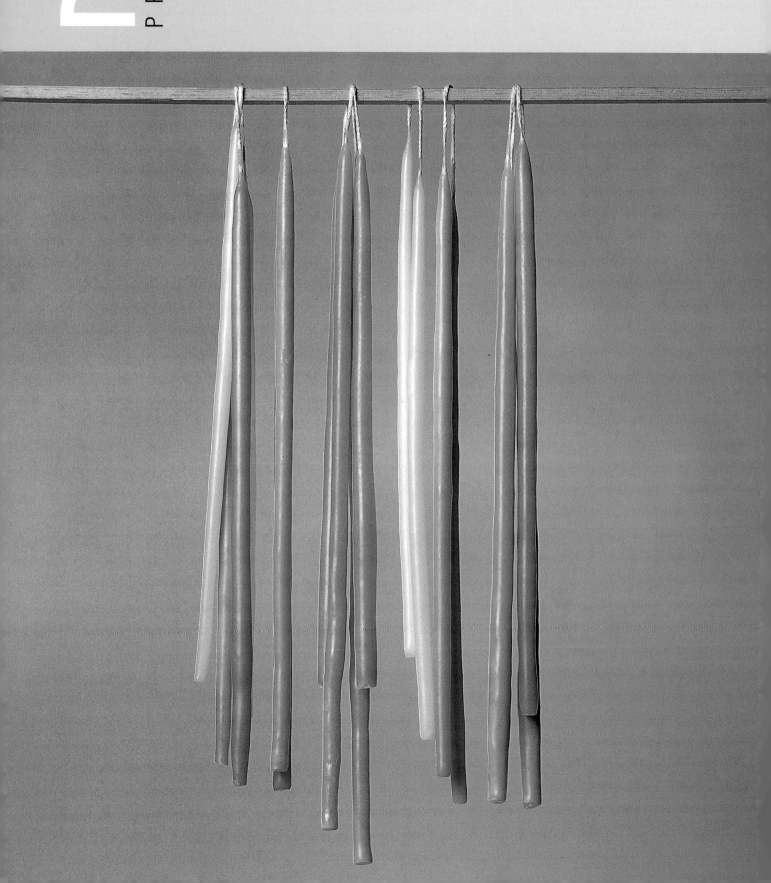

These traditionally dipped thin tapers look stunning when a selection in delicate shades of pastel colours is grouped together. This is a very simple method of candle making that does not require a mould.

You will need

625 g (1 lb 6 oz) paraffin wax

75 g (3 oz) stearin

Blue dye disc

Dipping can, 30 cm (12 in) tall

Saucepan

Wax thermometer

Double boiler

Knife

Spoon

Greaseproof paper

2 nails

Hammer

Piece of board (optional)

53 cm (21 in) length of 1.2 cm (½ in) wick (for each pair of tapers)

Kitchen towel

Scissors

1 Stand the dipping can in a saucepan of water. Put the paraffin wax into the can and heat to 82°C (180°F). Meanwhile, in a double boiler, heat the stearin to 82°C (180°F); stearin is not essential for making the tapers but it is a good idea to use it as it helps dissolve the dye and make the colour more opaque. With a knife, scrape a little of the blue dye disc into the stearin to colour it. Add only slithers of dye at a time to achieve a pale shade of blue, and stir.

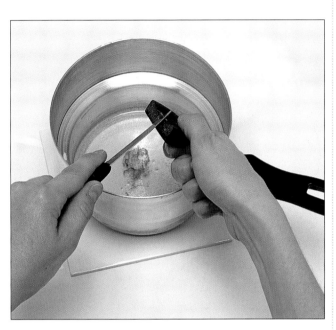

2 Pour the stearin into the wax in the dipping can and stir gently with the thermometer. Remove the can from the heat and allow the wax, stearin and dye mixture to cool to 71°C (160°F). Fix two nails to a wall or board, about 2.5 cm (1 in) apart. A pair of tapers can then hang over the nails while cooling. Fold the length of wick in half and hold it in the centre. Dip the wick into the mixture in the dipping can.

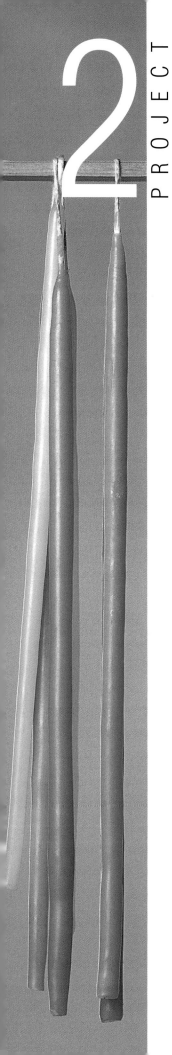

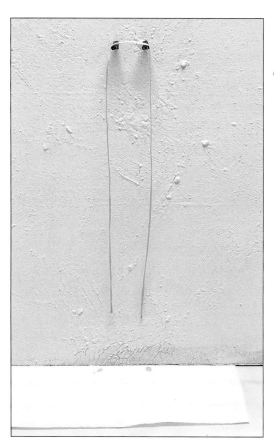

3 Lift out the wick after about 3 seconds and hang it across the nails. Lay a sheet of kitchen towel underneath to catch any drips of wax. Leave to cool for about 1 minute, then gently pull the ends of the wicks to straighten the tapers.

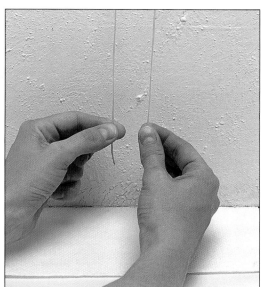

4 Check that the temperature of the wax remains at 71°C (160°F), and continue dipping the tapers into the wax and holding them there for 3 seconds, then hanging them to cool and harden for about 1 minute, until you achieve the desired thickness. These tapers are about 1 cm (⅜ in) in diameter.

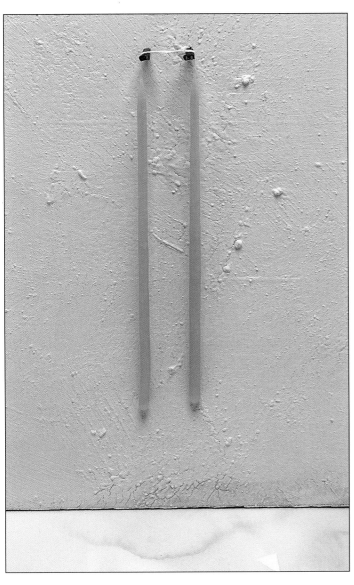

5 Finally, return the dipping can to the saucepan and heat the wax to 82°C (180°F). Give the tapers a final dip to produce a smooth finish and hang to cool as before.

artist's tip

You can create other pastel shades by adding small amounts of dye to the stearin. Try using a little pink dye, or mix small amounts of pink and blue dye together to make a lilac colour. Blue and yellow makes green, or add just a touch of yellow dye to make a creamy shade.

6 When the tapers have cooled and hardened completely, rest the pair on a wad of kitchen towels and carefully trim the ends with a knife. When you are ready to light the tapers, after at least 1 hour, cut the wick to separate the candles and trim to about 1.5 cm (⅝ in).

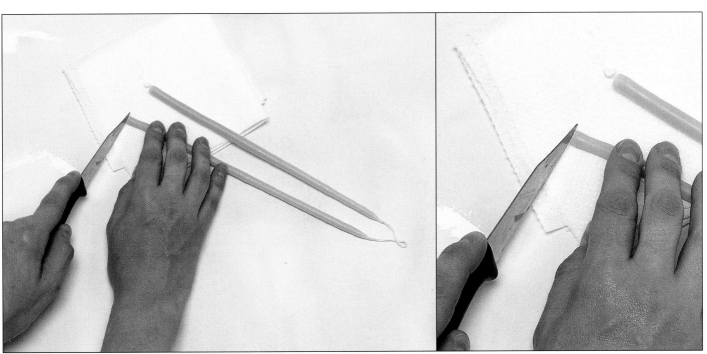

Scented candles release a delightful aroma to their surroundings when lit. It is a good idea to colour your candles to coordinate with their scents, so here we have made pink, rose-scented candles. Since these candles remain in their containers, there is no need to add stearin to the wax when making them.

You will need

150 g (6 oz) paraffin wax

Pink dye disc

Rose wax perfume

Small heatproof china container, 7 cm (2¾ in) diameter and 10 cm (4 in) tall

15 cm (6 in) length of small papercore wick

Small wick sustainer

Pliers

Wax glue

Marker pen

Knife

Cocktail stick

Double boiler

Wax thermometer

Spoon

Greaseproof paper

Needle

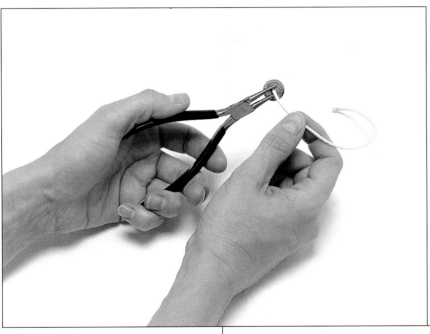

1 Heat up the china container with some warm water. Slip one end of the papercore wick into a wick sustainer. Squeeze the sustainer with a pair of pliers to hold the wick.

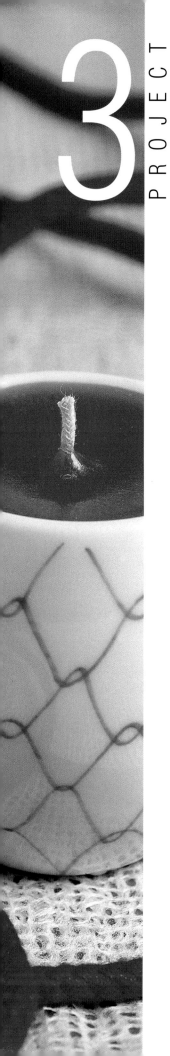
2 Spread wax glue on the underside of the sustainer with a knife. Fix the sustainer firmly in the centre of the china container. Make a small mark on the inside of the container, 6 mm (¼ in) below the top.

3 Rest a cocktail stick across the top of the container. Tie the wick around the stick so that it stands upright and central in the container.

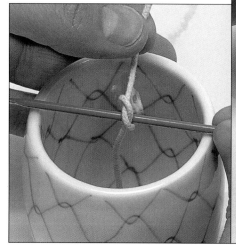

4 In a double boiler, heat the paraffin wax to 82°C (180°F). Cut off slithers of the dye disc and gradually add them to colour the wax. Stir gently. To test the colour, drop a little of the wax onto some greaseproof paper and leave to dry.

5 Check the temperature of the wax is still 82°C (180°F), then, when you are ready to pour, drop one or two drops of rose wax perfume into the mixture.

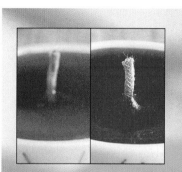

artist's tip

Pink wax is much stronger in colour when it has cooled than when molten, so add only very small amounts of dye at a time and keep testing the colour on greaseproof paper until you achieve the desired effect.

variation

You can make a pair of container candles in different shades of pink. Make two batches of pink wax, one stronger in colour than the other.

6 Pour the wax into the container up to the mark, retaining the excess wax for topping up. Leave for 1 hour, then prick the wax around the wick with a needle and top up the well to just below the previous poured level with wax at 82°C (180°F). Leave to cool completely, then trim the wick to 1.5 cm (⅝ in) long.

Container Candles
Gallery

Travel candle
A candle made in a lightweight metal container with a screw-on lid can be closed away safely when travelling and used on holidays.

Beaker and saucer
Colour wax a delicate shade of purple to complement a smart oriental beaker. Allow to cool, then stand the beaker on a matching saucer.

Coloured glass
A plain white candle highlights the effects of coloured glass, as with this lilac bowl.

Recycling
A single container can be used again and again to house a candle. Add stearin to the wax when making the container candle so that you can release it when you want to change it: the released candle can be used elsewhere.

Can-can
Recycle a metal can to use as a smart candle container. Do take care when handling the metal during the candle-making process however, since it will become quite hot.

Terracotta planter
Candles look very effective in terracotta containers, especially for outdoor use. Plug the hole in the base of a plant pot securely with mould seal before pouring in the wax.

Aromatic pine
Add the refreshing scent of pine wax perfume to green wax to make this candle in a small ceramic bowl.

Garden bowl
This rustic clay bowl is an ideal container for a candle to be used outdoors, it is low and heavy so will not fall over in a breeze.

Coloured cube
Coloured candles look wonderful in plain glass containers such as this chunky cube.

A glass dish was used as a mould to make this watery looking candle, delicately coloured using small amounts of pearl white and blue wax dye. This wide candle has three evenly spaced wicks that ensure it will burn brightly.

You will need

450 g (1 lb) paraffin wax
50 g (2 oz) stearin
Pearl white dye disc
Blue dye disc

Pair of compasses
Ruler
Paper
Scissors
Protractor
Wicking needle
2 double boilers
Wax thermometer
Heatproof glass dish, 15 cm (6 in) in diameter
25 cm (10 in) length of 4 cm (1½ in) wick
Knife
Spoon
Greaseproof paper

1 To make a template for evenly positioning the wicks, use a pair of compasses to describe a 14 cm (5½ in) diameter circle on paper. Cut out the circle then divide it into thirds using a protractor. Mark each division 3.5 cm (1⅜ in) from the centre. Use a wicking needle to pierce holes at the marks

2 Set a quarter of the paraffin wax and stearin aside. In a double boiler, heat the wax to 82°C (180°F). Dip the wick into the molten wax to prime it.

3 In the second double boiler, heat the stearin to 82°C (180°F). Cut off slithers of the pearl white dye disc and gradually add them to the stearin to whiten the wax. Pearl white dye discs are much harder to dissolve than other colours, so stir the stearin well to mix the dye. Add the wax to the stearin and stir gently. To test the colour, drop a little of the wax onto some greaseproof paper and leave to dry.

4 Pour the wax into the dish to a depth of approximately 3 cm (1¼ in). Empty any excess wax into a bowl lined with greaseproof paper and clean the two double boilers ready to prepare the blue wax. Allow the pearl white wax in the mould to cool for about 1¼ hours, until the wax feels rubbery to the touch.

5 Meanwhile, in a clean double boiler, heat the set aside wax to 82°C (180°F). In the second double boiler heat the set aside stearin to 82°C (180°F). Cut off slithers of the blue dye disc and add them to the stearin to make a pale blue shade. Add the wax to the stearin and stir. Pour the wax into the dish over the rubbery pearl white wax to a depth of about 1.2 cm (½ in).

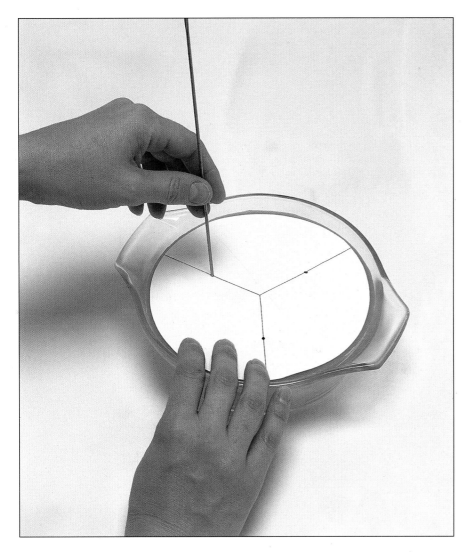

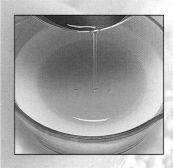

artist's tip

If the colours of the finished candle blend into each other, the first layer was not set enough when the second layer was poured in. This can create a beautiful effect in its own right, but if you want clearly defined stripes, make sure the whole of the first layer feels rubbery before you pour in the second.

6 When the blue top layer feels rubbery, place the paper template centrally over the candle and prick through the holes with the wicking needle to mark the wax underneath.

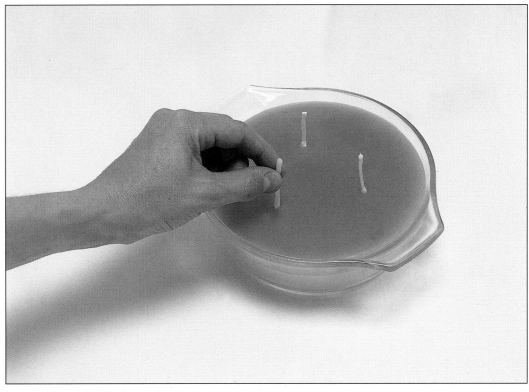

7 Remove the template and pierce the holes through both layers of wax. Cut three 8 cm (3¼ in) lengths of primed wick. Insert each length into a hole. Leave the candle to cool completely then tip it out of the mould. Trim the wicks to 1.5 cm (⅝ in) long.

Tall Triangle

T his slim, elegant candle is created using a triangular mould made from cardboard. The candle is embellished with copper metal leaf, which is available in books of sheets from art shops and specialist gilding suppliers.

You will need

270 g (9 oz) paraffin wax
30 g (1½ oz) stearin
Yellow dye disc
Transfer copper leaf

Thin card
Pen
Scissors
Thick card
Cutting mat
Craft knife
Metal ruler
Strong waterproof tape
2 double boilers
Wax thermometer
Knife
Spoon
Greaseproof paper
35 cm (14 in) length of 4 cm (1½ in) wick
Wicking needle
Mould seal
Support for candle, such as a dipping can
Needle
Scrap paper
Spray adhesive

1 To make the mould, transfer the triangle on page 92 onto thin card. Cut it out to use as a template. Place the template on some thick card and draw around it. Replace the template against one drawn edge and draw around it again. Repeat for a third time. On a cutting mat, cut out the whole shape along the outer edges with a craft knife and metal ruler.

2 Score along the inner lines with the craft knife and metal ruler. Bend the card along the scored lines. Butt the two long edges together and fix them securely together with strong waterproof tape. Snip off the tip of the mould so that the wick can poke through.

3 In a double boiler, heat the wax to 82°C (180°F). Dip the end 5 cm (2 in) of the wick into the molten wax to prime it. Allow to harden then poke about 3 cm (1¼ in) out of the hole from inside the mould. In the second double boiler, heat the stearin to 82°C (180°F). Shave off a little of the yellow dye disc and stir it into the stearin to make a creamy colour. Add the wax to the stearin and stir. To test the colour, drop a little of the wax onto some greaseproof paper and leave to dry.

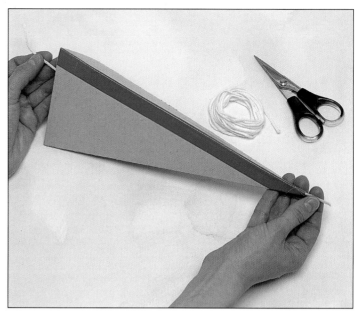

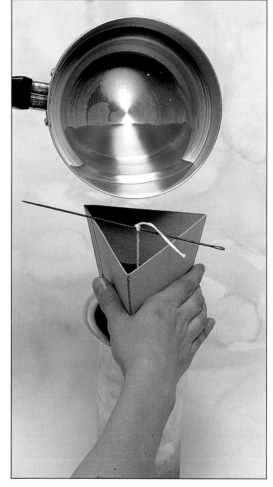

4 Rest a wicking needle across the upturned base of the mould and tie the other end of the wick tightly around it. Pull the wick taut and wrap mould seal securely around the primed end to prevent wax escaping.

5 Stand the mould in a dipping can or similar container to support it. Pour in the wax, retaining the excess for topping up. After a few minutes, tap the sides of the mould to release any trapped air bubbles.

6   Leave the wax to cool for about 1 hour, then use a needle to prick the wax around the wick where a well will have formed. Reheat the wax to 82°C (180°F) and top up the well to just below the previously poured level. Leave to cool completely then peel off the mould. Pull out the wicking needle and cut the wick at the base with scissors. Trim the wick at the top of the candle to 1.5 cm (⅝ in). Level the base in a heated saucepan (see page 15).

artist's tip

To make a shorter candle, simply pour in less wax. For an alternative decorative effect, wind metallic thread around the lower 4 cm (1½ in) of the candle. Then heat the excess wax to 82°C (180°F) and dip the decorated candle in the wax to the depth of the thread. Hold there for a few seconds and remove.

7   Lay a sheet of transfer copper leaf, right side up, on some scrap paper and lightly spray with spray adhesive.

8   Carefully cut triangles of copper leaf, holding the triangles by the edges to prevent the glued surface tearing or sticking to you. Place one triangle face down on the candle about 1 cm (⅜ in) above the base and gently press in place. Peel off the backing paper. Add more triangles around the base of the candle to achieve the desired effect.

Appliqué Effects
Gallery

Hooped candle
Bind strips of blue
appliqué wax, varying
in width, around a tall
silver candle, then butt
the ends together on
the back of the candle.

Striped candle
Punch a hole in the centre of three 2 cm
(¾ in) squares of holograph appliqué
wax and apply them in a row on the front
of a frosted candle (see pages 88–91).
Stick strips of plain and holographic
appliqué wax in stripes around the
remainder of the candle.

Spiral decoration
The spiral symbolizes creative energy
and so this candle would make a
great gift for a keen crafter.

Harlequin style
A tall crystal candle
has gold appliqué wax
diamonds applied
along its length.

Spiral candle
A tall blue candle
has silver appliqué
spirals positioned
down its length.

Astrology additions
This cool blue candle
is decorated with
astrological water
signs using appliqué
wax. Apply the other
zodiac signs to candles
in appropriate colours.

Chequerboard
Stick 1.5 cm (⅜ in)
squares of blue
appliqué wax to a
gold candle to create
this chequerboard
style effect.

6 PROJECT Layers of Colour

P retty hoops of colour are created by pouring different shades of wax into a mould one after the other, when the previous colour is almost set. Here different shades of the same colour have been used but you could use a range of different colours.

1 To prepare the mould, stick a length of masking tape along the height of one side. Starting from the base of the mould, which will become the top of the candle, use a ballpoint pen to mark off four lines at 3 cm (1¼ in) intervals for the stripes.

2 In a double boiler, heat the wax to 82°C (180°F). In the second double boiler, heat the stearin to 82°C (180°F). With a knife, scrape a little red dye into the stearin for the first colour, which will be the palest and gently stir. Add the wax to the stearin and mix well. Divide into four approximately equal amounts and pour them into separate heatproof containers.

You will need

360 g (13 oz) paraffin wax

40 g (2 oz) stearin

Red dye disc

Square plastic candle mould, 6 cm (2⅜ in) wide and 16 cm (6½ in) tall

Masking tape

Scissors

Ballpoint pen

Ruler

2 double boilers

Wax thermometer

Knife

Spoon

4 heatproof containers

Greaseproof paper

25 cm (10 in) length of 5 cm (2 in) wick

Cocktail stick

Mould seal

Water bath

Weight

Needle

6

3 Set one wax aside. Add more dye to the remaining waxes to colour each one slightly darker than the last. Test all four waxes by pouring a little of each onto greaseproof paper. Allow the samples to cool and harden. This will give you an idea of how they will look when set. Make sure each colour looks sufficiently different from its neighbour.

4 Reheat the palest coloured wax that was set aside. Dip the wick into the molten wax to prime it. Allow the wick to harden then, from the inside, push about 3 cm (1¼ in) out of the hole at the base of the mould. Rest a cocktail stick across the open top of the mould and tie the other end of the wick tightly around it. At the base of the mould, pull the wick taut and secure it in place with mould seal. Pour in the first colour up to the first mark on the mould. After a few minutes, tap the side of the mould to release any air bubbles. Stand the mould in a bowl of water with a weight on top.

5 Leave the candle for approximately 45 minutes. Check that the first layer has hardened around the edge but is still rubbery in the centre by gently pressing it. Heat the second colour, the second lightest shade, to 82°C (180°F). Carefully pour it into the mould, up to the second mark. After a few minutes, tap the side of the mould to release any air bubbles. Return the mould to the water bath.

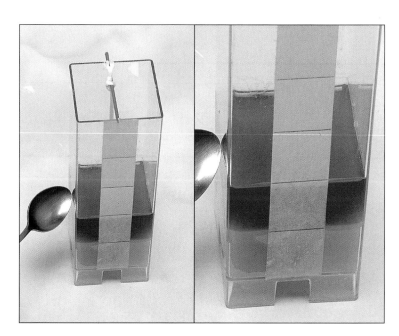

6 Leave the candle to partially set and check it as before. Heat the third colour to 82°C (180°F) and pour it into the mould up to the third mark. After a few minutes, tap the side of the mould and return it to the water bath.

7 Allow the candle to partially set as before. Heat the fourth and final colour to 82°C (180°F) and pour it into the mould, up to the last mark, retaining the excess for topping up. After a few minutes, tap the side of the mould and return it to the water bath. Leave for 1 hour then use a needle to prick the wax around the wick where a well will have formed. Reheat the extra wax to 82°C (180°F) and top up the well to just below the previous poured level. Leave to cool completely in the water bath.

8 Remove the mould seal and slip the candle out of the mould. Pull out the cocktail stick and cut the wick level with the base of the candle with scissors. Trim the wick at the top to 1.5 cm (⅝ in).

variation

Create a diagonally striped candle by holding the mould at an angle when pouring in the wax. The mould must be supported at the same angle when you place it in the water bath, or the effect will be lost.

7 PROJECT Floating Flowers

Special occasions merit special candles and these lovely flowers make a stunning display when floating in water. This project uses dip and carve wax to model the petals, and the quantity described here will make at least four candles. It is a good idea to colour all the wax first then make one candle at a time.

You will need

200 g (7 oz) dip and carve wax
Yellow dye disc
Blue dye disc
Pink dye disc

2 double boilers
Wax thermometer
20 cm (8 in) length of 1.2 cm (½ in) wick
Knife
Spoon
Greaseproof paper
Ruler
Scissors
Baking foil
Wax glue

1 In a double boiler, heat one-quarter of the dip and carve wax to 82°C (180°F). Dip the wick into the wax to prime it. Leave the wick to harden then cut 5 cm (2 in) lengths for each candle. Shave off a little of the yellow dye disc and stir it into the wax. To test the colour, drop a little of the wax onto some greaseproof paper and leave to dry. In the second double boiler, heat the rest of the dip and carve wax to 82°C (180°F). Add a little each of the blue and pink dyes and stir them into the wax to colour it lilac.

2 Cut an 11 cm (4¼ in) square of baking foil. Fold the edges up to make a shallow tray, about 1 cm (⅜ in) deep, to hold the wax. Fold the corners tightly so the wax cannot escape. Make another tray in the same way using a 15 cm (6 in) square of baking foil. Photocopy or trace the small and large petal templates on page 92 and cut out.

3 Pour the yellow wax into the small tray to a depth of about 3 mm (⅛ in). Pour the lilac wax into the large tray to the same depth. Retain the excess wax in the double boilers. Allow the wax to cool slightly and become rubbery. Place the small petal template on the yellow wax and cut around it with a knife.

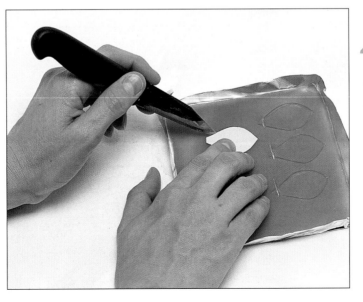

4 Place the large petal template in the corner of the lilac wax square and cut around it with a knife. Repeat to cut five large petals.

5 Lay a wick vertically down the length of the yellow petal and wrap the base of the petal over the end of the wick to secure it. Bend the rest of the petal shape outwards slightly so that it will not get caught by the flame when the candle is lit.

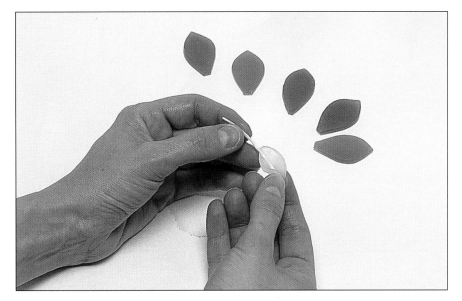

6 Dab a little wax glue on the straight end of one large petal. Wrap it around the small yellow petal. Bend the body of the petal outwards and bend the tip upwards. Arrange and glue the remaining large petals around the small petal, bending them outwards. Set the candle aside to cool completely.

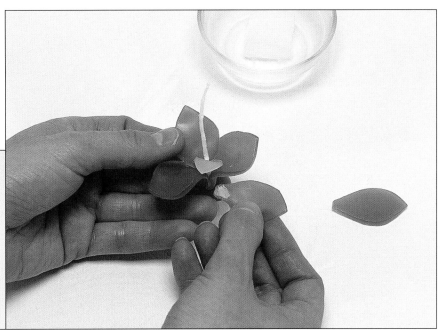

7 Reheat the remaining lilac wax to 82°C (180°F) in the double boiler and remove it from the heat. Hold the flower firmly by the wick and dip the base of the flower into the wax to seal it. Allow the excess wax to drip back into the double boiler. Trim the wick to 1.5 cm (⅝ in) before lighting.

candle making/project 7

Button Embedded Candle

P retty mother-of-pearl buttons have been captured within this candle. It is an intriguing technique and bound to make those not "in the know" ask how it is done, but you don't have to tell them how easy it is.

You will need

360 g (12½ oz) paraffin wax
40 g (2½ oz) stearin
Blue dye disc
Mother-of-pearl buttons

2 double boilers
Wax thermometer
21 cm (8⅜ in) length of 6 cm (2½ in) wick
Knife
Spoon
Greaseproof paper
Round plastic candle mould, 6.5 cm (2½ in) diameter and 13 cm (5⅛ in) tall
Mould seal
Wicking needle
Masking tape (optional)
Scissors
Water bath
Weight
Needle
Domestic iron
Kitchen towel

1 In a double boiler, heat the wax to 82°C (180°F). Dip the end 5 cm (2 in) of the wick into the molten wax to prime it. In the second double boiler heat the stearin to 82°C (180°F). Cut off slithers of the blue dye disc and gradually stir them into the stearin to produce a sky blue colour. Add the wax to the stearin and gently stir. To test the colour, drop a little of the wax onto some greaseproof paper and leave to dry.

2 Allow the wick to harden then poke about 3 cm (1¼ in) of the primed end out of the hole from inside the mould. Hold the wick in place with mould seal. Rest a wicking needle across the shoulder of the mould and tie the other end of the wick tightly around it. Pull the wick taut and press the mould seal securely around the primed end to prevent the wax escaping.

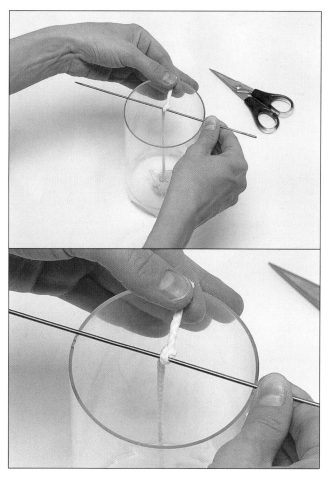

3 Pour the wax into the mould to a depth of about 8 cm (3¼ in). You might like to mark this measurement on the outside of the mould with masking tape. After about 5 minutes, pour the wax back into the double boiler. A thin layer of wax will remain in the mould.

4 Working quickly before the wax cools, press two rows of buttons firmly into the wax about 1 cm (⅜ in) from what will be the base of the candle. Knock the wicking needle to one side if it gets in the way. Reposition the needle when the buttons are in place and make sure the wick is central.

5 Allow the wax in the double boiler to cool to 73°C (165°F) and pour it back into the mould up to the previously poured level. The wax needs to have cooled so that it does not melt the first layer holding the buttons. Keep the excess wax for topping up. After 1 minute, tap the side of the mould to release any air bubbles. Stand the mould in a water bath with a weight on top.

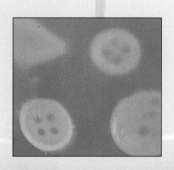

artist's tip

You can also experiment with the embedding technique using other small items such as shells, glass pebbles, beads or dried flowers, fruit or leaves. But always remember, after embedding the items, to pour the wax back at 73°C (165°F), not the original 82°C (180°F).

6 Leave for 1 hour then prick the wax around the wick where a well will have formed. Reheat the wax to 82°C (180°F) and top up the well to just below the previously poured level. Leave to cool completely in the water bath then remove the mould seal and slip the candle out of the mould. Pull out the wicking needle and cut the wick at the base with a pair of scissors. Trim the wick at the top of the candle to 1.5 cm (⅝ in). To level the base, gently heat an iron and hold the candle against the heated surface. Wipe the iron clean immediately with kitchen towels.

Oriental Painted Candle

The dramatic oriental imagery on this chunky pillar candle means "happy" in Chinese and will, hopefully, evoke a joyful mood wherever you choose to place it. The design is painted onto the surface of the finished candle with acrylic paint. This is a great technique to use to add a personal touch to plain candles.

You will need

540 g (1 lb 3 oz) paraffin wax
60 g (2 oz) stearin
Brown dye disc
Red dye disc
Cream acrylic paint

2 double boilers
Wax thermometer
21 cm (8⅜ in) length of 6 cm (2⅜ in) wick
Knife
Spoon
Greaseproof paper
Round plastic candle mould, 6.5 cm (2½ in) diameter and 13 cm (5⅛ in) tall
Wicking needle
Mould seal
Water bath
Weight
Needle
Scissors
Sharp pencil
Thin paper
Kitchen towel
Masking tape
Artist's paintbrush
Dry duster

1 In a double boiler, heat the wax to 82°C (180°F). Dip the end 5 cm (2 in) of the wick into the molten wax to prime it. In the second double boiler, heat the stearin to 82°C (180°F). Slice the brown dye disc in half. Crush one half with the back of a spoon and stir it into the stearin. Shave off a little of the red dye disc and add it to the mixture. Add the wax to the stearin and mix thoroughly. To test the colour, drop a little of the wax onto some greaseproof paper and leave to dry.

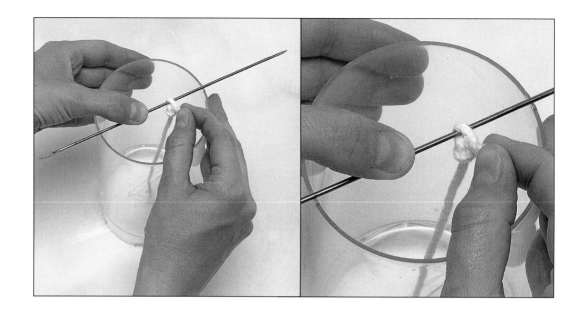

2 Allow the wick to harden then poke about 3 cm (1¼ in) of the primed end out of the hole from inside the mould. Rest a wicking needle across the open top of the mould, which will become the base of the candle, and tie the other end of the wick tightly around it.

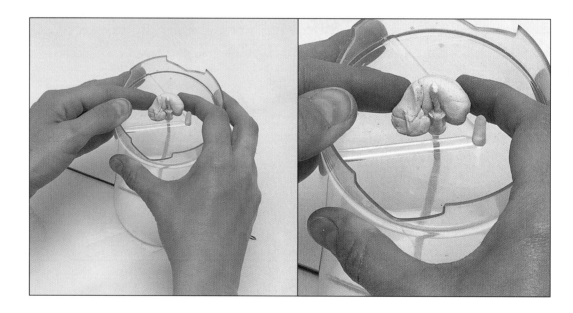

3 Pull the wick taut and wrap mould seal securely around the primed wick to prevent the wax escaping.

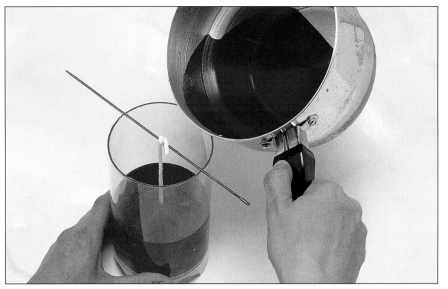

4 Pour the wax into the mould and keep the excess for topping up. After a few minutes, tap the side of the mould to release any air bubbles. Stand the mould in a water bath with a weight on top. Leave for 1 hour, then use a needle to prick the wax around the wick where a well will have formed. Reheat the excess wax to 82°C (180°F) and top up the well to just below the previously poured level. Leave to cool completely in the water bath. Remove the mould seal and slip the candle out of the mould. Pull out the wicking needle and cut the wick level with the base of the candle with scissors. Trim the primed wick at the top to 1.5 cm (⅝ in).

5 Trace the oriental design on page 93 onto a piece of thin paper to use as a template. Rest the candle on a few sheets of kitchen towel to protect it, and tape the template to the front of the candle. Firmly redraw the motif to transfer it to the candle. Keep the pencil sharpened or use a propelling pencil to lightly indent the wax. Peel off the tape and remove the template.

6 Paint in the design using cream acrylic paint and an artist's paintbrush. Leave to dry. To finish, gently buff the candle with a dry duster.

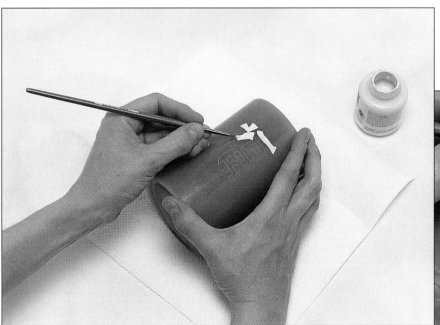

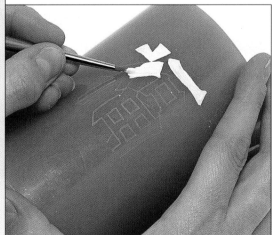

Floating Candles
Gallery

Petit four boats
Use petit four
cookery moulds to
make a set of floating
boat candles. Pour the
wax into the mould then add
the primed wick when the wax is
rubbery but not completely set. To
prevent water seepage, make sure
the hole does not go completely
through the wax.

Leaves
These oak leaves are cut
from wax poured in a
baking tray. Score
veins on the surface
with a knife before
the wax cools.

Stars
Use cookie cutters to stamp wax that has been poured into a baking tray. Stamp the candles when the wax is rubbery but not completely set. Pierce a hole for the wick but not right through the wax, the wick must not be able to draw up water while floating. Insert a primed wick and leave to cool.

Daisies
Use dip and carve wax to model these pretty florals. The round discs in the centre are applied with wax glue.

Glitter hearts
Pour wax into a baking tray then scatter glitter on the surface after 5 minutes, when the wax starts to cool. Use heart-shaped cookie cutters when the wax is rubbery but not completely set. Shake off the excess glitter when the candles have cooled.

Orchids
These exotic flower candles are created with two shades of pink wax following the instructions on pages 46–49.

Quivering jelly wax is a wonderfully tactile material that is displayed at its best in a transparent container. Here, an inexpensive glass tumbler is decorated with gold ceramic paint to coordinate with the warm red colouring of the jelly wax.

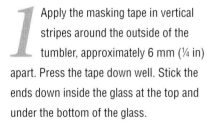

You will need

Gold ceramic paint

340 g (12 oz) jelly wax

Red powder wax dye

2.5 cm (1 in) wide masking tape

Scissors

Heatproof tumbler, 8 cm (3¼ in) diameter and 10 cm (4 in) tall

Kitchen towel

1.2 cm (½ in) flat paintbrush

15 cm (6 in) length of small papercore wick

Large wick sustainer

Pliers

Wax glue

Knife

Wicking needle

Double boiler

Wax thermometer

Spoon

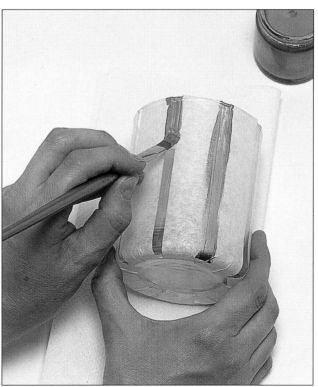

1 Apply the masking tape in vertical stripes around the outside of the tumbler, approximately 6 mm (¼ in) apart. Press the tape down well. Stick the ends down inside the glass at the top and under the bottom of the glass.

2 Lay the glass on its side on a few sheets of kitchen towel so it does not roll around. Apply gold ceramic paint between the masking tape on the uppermost area of the glass. Leave to dry, then turn the glass to continue painting the stripes. Allow to dry then apply a second coat of paint.

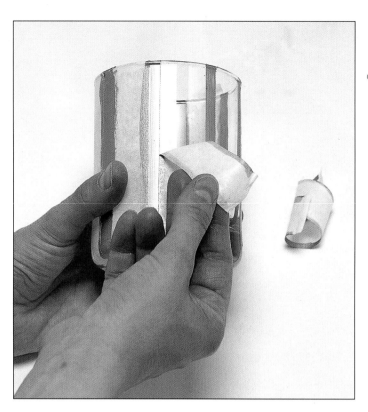

3 Leave the tumbler to dry completely then carefully peel off the masking tape to reveal the stripes.

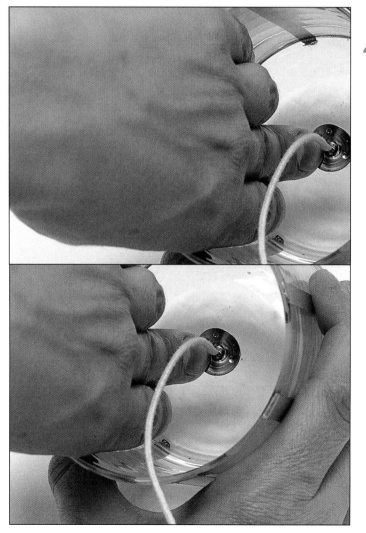

4 Insert one end of the papercore wick into a wick sustainer and squeeze the sustainer closed with a pair of pliers, enclosing the wick. Make sure the glass is dry inside and out. Spread wax glue on the underside of the sustainer and stick the sustainer firmly in the centre of the tumbler.

5 Rest a wicking needle across the top of the tumbler and tie the wick securely around it so that the wick stands taut and upright in the centre of the tumbler.

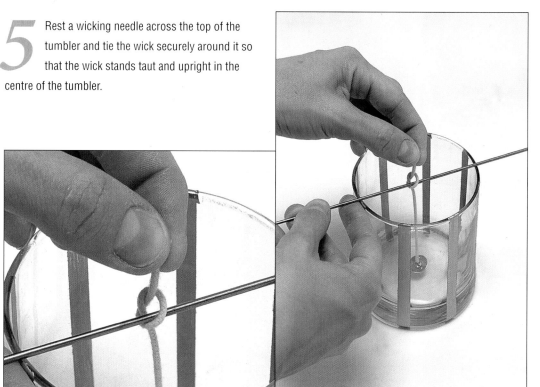

artist's tip

The colour of molten jelly wax does not change when the wax sets. So the colour of the wax in the pan truthfully describes the colour the finished candle will be.

6 Heat the jelly wax in a double boiler to 110°C (215°F). Pick up a very small amount of the powder wax dye on the tip of a knife and sprinkle it into the wax. Stir to dissolve it completely. Only a tiny amount of powder is needed to produce a strong colour, so use it very sparingly.

7 Pour the wax into the tumbler to about 1 cm (⅜ in) below the rim. Leave to cool. Pull out the wicking needle and cut the wick to 1.5 cm (⅝ in) long.

Stacked Triangles

This geometric candle with its alternating bands of deep brown and cream stripes is created by cutting triangles of wax and then threading them onto a primed wick. You can use any two colours that contrast well with each other.

You will need

720 g (1lb 9 oz) paraffin wax

80 g (4 oz) stearin

Brown dye disc

Black dye disc

Yellow dye disc

Scissors

Masking tape

Ruler

Round baking tray, 20 cm (8 in) diameter

2 double boilers

Wax thermometer

Knife

Spoon

Greaseproof paper

Wicking needle

Craft knife

15 cm (6 in) length of 4 cm (1½ in) wick

Small wick sustainer

Pliers

1 Stick a piece of masking tape on the inside edge of the baking tray, about 1.5 cm (⅝ in) up from the base. Divide the quantities of wax and stearin in half. In a double boiler heat one half of the wax to 82°C (180°F). In the second double boiler heat one half of the stearin to 82°C (180°F).

2 Crush half the brown and one-quarter of the black dye discs with a spoon and stir them into the stearin to make a dark brown colour. Add the heated wax to the stearin and stir. To test the colour, drop a little of the wax onto some greaseproof paper and leave to dry.

3 Pour the wax into the baking tray to the level of the tape. Set the tray aside to cool for 45 minutes.

4 Photocopy or trace the triangle template on page 93 and cut it out. Pierce the dot in the centre with a wicking needle. When the wax has partially cooled and is rubbery to the touch, place the template on the wax and cut around it with a craft knife, holding the knife blade upright. Mark the holes with the wicking needle. Repeat to cut three triangles.

5 Use the wicking needle to pierce the holes through to the base of the tray: they should be large enough to take the wick. Leave to cool completely then tip out the triangles.

6 Clean the tray and double boilers, ready for the next batch of wax. In one double boiler, heat the put aside wax to 82°C (180°F). Meanwhile, in the second double boiler, heat the set aside stearin to 82°C (180°F). Shave off a little of the yellow dye disc and add it to the stearin to make a creamy colour. Add the wax to the stearin and mix well. Dip the wick into the wax to prime it. Pour the wax into the tray and follow Steps 3–5 to make three cream triangles with holes in their centres.

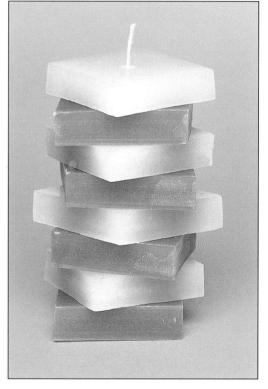

7 When the primed wick has cooled, slip one end into a wick sustainer. Squeeze the sustainer with pliers to hold the wick securely in place. Thread the triangles onto the wick then arrange each piece at a slightly different angle to achieve the desired effect. Trim the wick to 1.5 cm (⅝ in).

variation

A diamond template was used to cut these layers, producing a variation on the stacked theme. The white layers were made by colouring the wax with a pearl white dye disc.

This pretty shell stencilled lantern looks delightful with a nightlight inside and is just the thing for a twilight alfresco supper. A waxed card drink carton is used as a mould, then pretty shells are stencilled on the set candle's walls with spray paint.

You will need

750 g (1lb 10 oz) paraffin wax
Blue spray paint

Large waxed card drink carton
Ruler
Pen
Scissors
Double boiler
Wax thermometer
Knife
Stencil card
Craft knife
Cutting mat
Masking tape
Scrap paper

1 Empty the drink carton and cut it 12 cm (4¾ in) above the base. Wash and dry it thoroughly. In a double boiler, heat the paraffin wax to 82°C (180°F). Pour the wax into the carton.

2 Leave the wax to cool until it forms a skin on the top and sides about 6 mm (¼ in) thick. Use a knife to cut off the top layer of wax, and return it to the double boiler.

3 Pour the still-molten wax in the carton into the double boiler, leaving four walls and a base of partially solid wax.

4 Leave the lantern to cool, then tear off the carton to reveal it. Level the base if necessary in a heated saucepan (see page 15). Level the top edge in the same way.

5 Use the template on page 93 to draw shells onto stencil card. Cut out the stencil with a craft knife, resting on a cutting mat.

artist's tip

To create a light, delicate look, use the spray paint sparingly. One short burst will produce an array of fine dots. To create more well-defined shapes, spray the same area with about three or four bursts, always leaving the paint for a minute or two between sprays to dry.

6 Tape the stencil to one side of the lantern with masking tape. Protect the surrounding area and the other sides of the lantern with scrap paper. Lightly spray the stencil with spray paint. Leave to dry then untape the stencil. Repeat on the other sides of the lantern.

Wrapped Candles
Gallery

Eucalyptus addition
Tie a sprig of artificial eucalyptus to
a tall candle with a length of string.

Bead trimming
Thread beads onto narrow organza
ribbon and wrap it around a candle,
sticking the ends to the back of the
candle with wax glue.

Waxed leaf tag
Pour a little green wax onto baking
foil then cut it into a leaf shape to
make a gift tag. Pierce a hole and
indent the veins with a knife tip. Tie
the leaf to the candle with raffia.

Copper plaque
Wrap a strip of frayed hessian around a candle.
Emboss a rectangle of copper leaf with a ballpoint pen
and glue it to the hessian (see pages 36–39).

Bay leaf bundle
Tie four candles together with raffia then slip a bay leaf
under the fastening as a finishing touch when giving
the candles as a present.

Cinnamon stick triangle
Tie a trio of cinnamon sticks to a triangular
frosted candle (see pages 88–91) using
two lengths of organza ribbon.

Chilli peppers wrapping
Wrap a chunky candle in iridescent film for
protection. Pierce a hole through the stalks
of three dried chillies and thread them onto
paper ribbon. Tie the chilli ribbon around
the film, enclosing the candle.

Dried fruit decoration
Thread a slice of dried fruit onto some fine leather thong
and tie it around the top of a double wick candle.

Christmas Tree Candle

T his three-dimensional festive tree candle will make a wonderful addition to your usual Christmas decorations. Two tree shapes are cut from wax that has been poured into a shallow tray. They are then cut in half and joined with wax glue, forming a cross that enables the tree to stand upright. Metal star studs provide understated embellishments.

You will need

360 g (12½ oz) paraffin wax
40g (1½ oz) stearin
Green dye disc
8 metal star studs

Masking tape
Ruler
Scissors
Round baking tray, 20 cm (8 in) diameter
2 double boilers
Wax thermometer
13 cm (5⅛ in) length of 1.2 cm (½ in) wick
Spoon
Pencil
Craft knife
Wicking needle
Small wick sustainer
Pliers
Wax glue

1 Stick a piece of masking tape on the inside edge of the baking tray, 1.2 cm (½ in) up from the base. In a double boiler heat the wax to 82°C (180°F). Dip the wick into the wax to prime it, and leave to harden.

2 In the second double boiler, heat the stearin to 82°C (180°F). Crush half the green dye disc with a spoon and stir it into the stearin. Add the wax to the stearin and mix well. Pour the wax into the tray up to the masking tape mark.

3 Leave the wax to cool for 45 minutes. Photocopy or trace the template on page 93 and cut it out. When the wax has cooled but is still warm and pliable, place the template on top of it and cut around it with a craft knife, holding the blade upright. Pierce the dots with a wicking needle. Cut the tree in half lengthwise. Repeat to cut another tree.

4 Press a metal star stud into the pierced dots on each tree section. Leave the wax to cool completely, then tip out the tree sections. Push a stud into the back of the trees matching the position of those on the front.

5 Slip one end of the wick into a wick sustainer. Squeeze the sustainer around the wick with a pair of pliers to secure it in position.

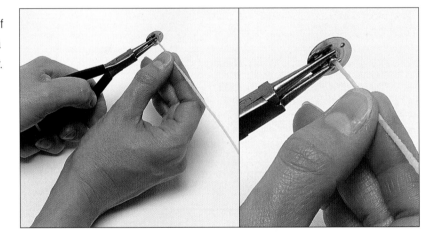

6 Cut a shallow "V" along the long, cut edges of two of the tree halves to create a channel to conceal the wick.

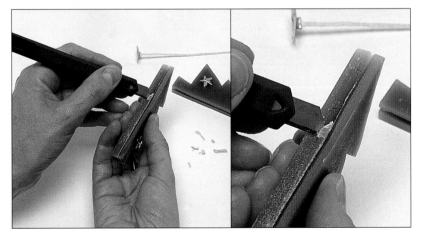

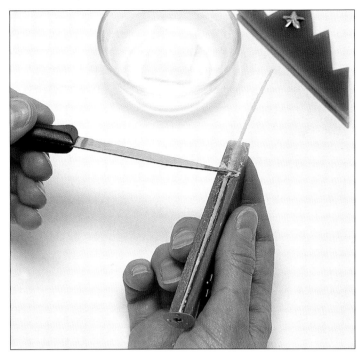

7 Press the wick into the channel of one of the tree halves, aligning the sustainer with the base of the tree. Spread wax glue over the cut edge of the tree section, covering the wick.

8 Take the second tree half with a channel cut into it, and press it together with the tree section containing the wick.

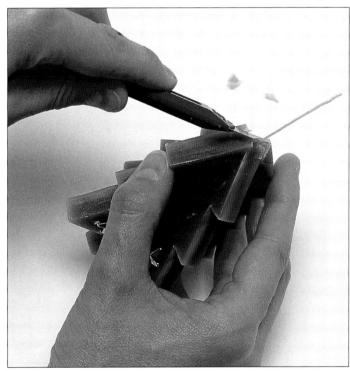

9 Spread wax glue on the long, cut edges of the remaining two half tree sections. Press these sections to the whole tree candle, covering the central join.

10 Carefully cut each side at the top of the tree sections you have just applied at an angle with the craft knife. Trim the wick to 1.5 cm (⅝ in).

reate an exotic atmosphere in the garden with a set of tall, patterned flares, perfect for summer barbecues or outdoor parties. The animal prints are made by cutting shapes from appliqué wax and sticking them onto the flares, which started out as humble bamboo canes.

You will need

800 g (2 lb) paraffin wax
Pearl white dye disc
Yellow dye disc
Brown dye disc
Red dye disc
Black appliqué wax
Brown appliqué wax
Brown parcel paper
Scissors
Ruler
Bamboo cane
Wax glue
Knife
Dipping can
Double boiler
Wax thermometer
Spoon
Support for the cane while drying, such as a dishwashing bowl
Kitchen towels
35 cm (14 in) length of 7.5 cm (3 in) wick
Pen
Cutting mat
Craft knife

1 Cut a strip of brown parcel paper 45 x 4 cm (18 x 1½ in). Stick the end of the strip diagonally to one end of a bamboo cane with wax glue. Bind the strip diagonally around the end 17 cm (7 in) of the cane and fix the end in place with wax glue. Cut off the excess strip. Tuck the top end of the strip into the cane.

2 Place the paraffin wax in a dipping can and stand the can in a double boiler. Heat the wax to 71°C (160°F). To make the zebra flare, add slithers of pearl white dye disc to the wax to whiten it. To make the leopard and giraffe flares, crush half a yellow dye disc and a quarter of a brown dye disc with a spoon and add to the wax to colour it. To make the tiger flare, crush half a yellow dye disc and a quarter of a red dye disc with a spoon and add to the wax to make an orange shade.

3 Dip the paper covered end of the cane into the wax. Lift the cane out after 3 seconds. Rest the uncovered part of the cane across a dishwashing bowl or similar, with kitchen towels in place to catch any drips of wax.

4 Leave to cool for 1 minute. Continue dipping the covered end of the cane in the wax for 3 seconds and leaving it to cool for 1 minute until the wax is 2.5 cm (1 in) thick. If the depth of the wax in the can is now lower than the wax on the cane, simply pour in more wax and reheat to 71°C (160°F).

5 Dip the wick in the wax to prime it, and allow the wick to cool. Starting at the bottom of the waxed area of cane, bind the wick diagonally around the wax. Allow the wick to extend at the top. Stick the ends in place with wax glue.

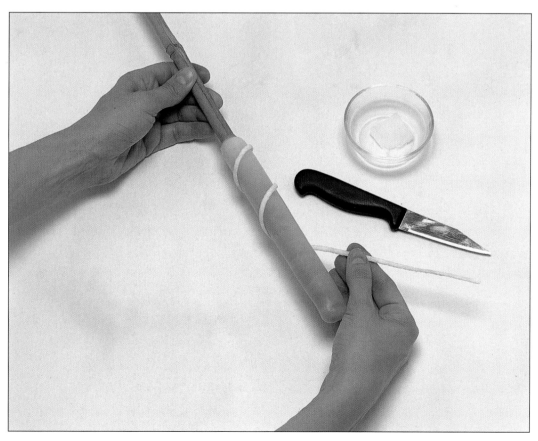

6 Continue dipping the cane as before until it has a fairly even finish. Do not worry if slight bumps over the wick are visible. The fur-effect animal markings will detract from them.

7 Photocopy or trace the desired animal print motif on page 94 and cut out the shapes. Draw around the shapes onto the backing paper of the appliqué wax: black appliqué wax for the zebra, leopard and tiger marks, brown appliqué wax for the second leopard marks and the giraffe print. Working over a cutting mat, use a craft knife to cut out the shapes, cutting through the wax.

8 Peel off the backing paper. Arrange the black pieces on the flares and press them firmly in place: position the zebra markings diagonally on the white flare and the tiger markings diagonally on the orange flare.

9 Place the black leopard markings on another yellow flare and then follow with the brown markings within the large black pieces. Place the brown giraffe markings on a plain yellow flare.

U nusual marble effects are created when two shades of dip and carve wax are blended together. Dip and carve wax can be moulded and shaped when it is warm. Cut the blended wax into a simple slab shape – this will show the realistic marbling effect at its best.

You will need

360 g (12½ oz) dip and carve wax

Black dye disc

Scissors

Ruler

Baking foil

Double boiler

Wax thermometer

6 cm (2⅜ in) length of 6.5 cm (2½ in) wick

Knife

Greaseproof paper

Hair-dryer (optional)

Rolling pin

Metal ruler

Wicking needle

Large wick sustainer

Pliers

1 Cut three 15 cm (6 in) squares of baking foil. Fold the edges upwards to make shallow trays – no more than 1.5 cm (⅝ in) deep – to hold the wax. Fold the corners tightly so wax cannot escape.

2 Heat the dip and carve wax in a double boiler to 82°C (180°F). Dip the wick into the wax to prime it and leave to cool and harden. Pour approximately one-third of the wax into each of two of the baking foil containers.

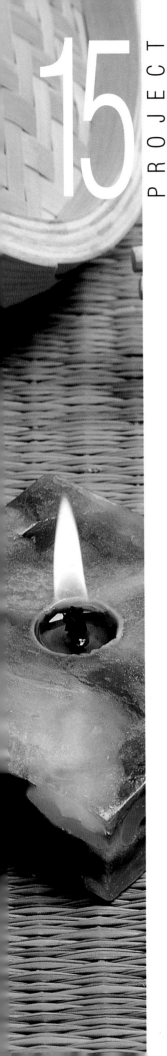

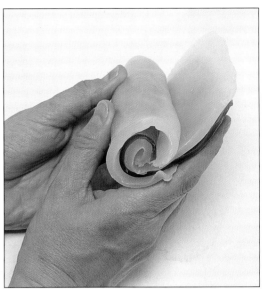

3 Add slithers of a black dye disc to the remaining wax in the double boiler. To test the colour, drop a little of the wax onto some greaseproof paper and leave to dry. When you are happy with the colour, pour it into the last foil container. Leave the sheets of wax to cool until rubbery, then peel off the foil.

4 Sandwich the black wax sheet between the two white wax sheets and roll them together.

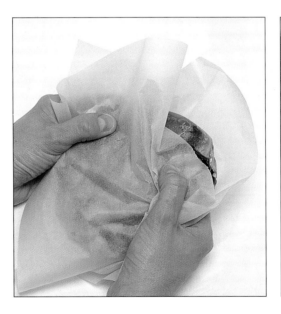

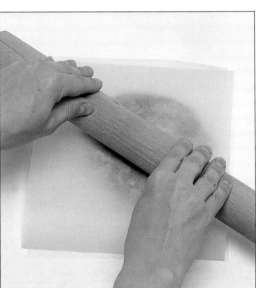

5 Place the rolled wax between two sheets of greaseproof paper and knead firmly to blend the colours. Work quickly before the wax sets: if it does become too hard to handle, warm the wax with a hair-dryer.

6 Place the wax between two clean sheets of greaseproof paper and use a rolling pin to roll it out to 2.5 cm (1 in) thick.

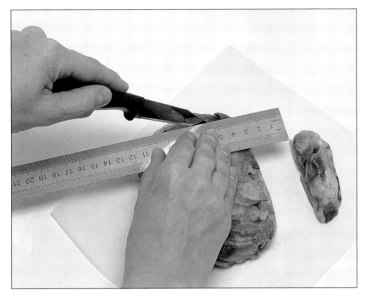

7 Remove the top layer of greaseproof paper. Use a knife against a metal ruler to cut the rolled wax into an 8 cm (3¼ in) square.

8 Pierce a hole in the centre of the marble slab with a wicking needle. Leave the candle to cool. Insert the wick into a wick sustainer and squeeze the sustainer with pliers to hold the wick in place.

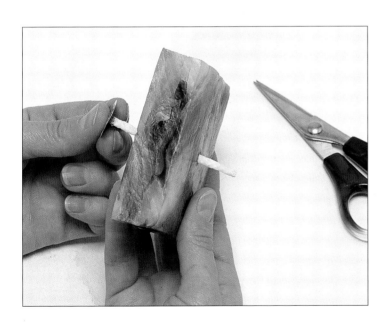

9 Insert the wick through the hole in the marble slab. Trim the wick to 1.5 cm (⅝ in) long.

variation

Any shades of dip and carve wax can be mixed together to create all manner of effects. Try two tones of yellow for a sienna marble look, or use vibrant colours, like this pink, to create a purely fantasy marble.

This unusual finish is achieved by allowing the wax to cool and then stirring it to produce a frothy texture. The finished candles will be paler in colour than those created with a traditional method so bear that in mind when colouring the wax. The wax, stearin and dye quantities here will make one lilac candle.

You will need

270 g (9 oz) paraffin wax

30 g (1½ oz) stearin

Blue dye disc

Pink dye disc

2 double boilers

Wax thermometer

18 cm (7 in) length of 5 cm (2 in) wick

Round plastic candle mould, 6 cm (2¼ in) diameter and 10 cm (4 in) tall

Cocktail stick

Mould seal

Knife

Spoon

Greaseproof paper

Scissors

Fork

Water bath

Weight

Needle

1 In a double boiler heat the wax to 82°C (180°F). Dip the end 5 cm (2 in) of the wick into the wax to prime it. Allow the wick to harden then poke about 3 cm (1¼ in) out of the hole from inside the mould. Rest a cocktail stick across the shoulder of the mould, which will become the base of the candle, and tie the other end around it. Pull the wick taut and secure the primed end around the hole with mould seal. In the second double boiler, heat the stearin to 82°C (180°F). Use a knife to scrape blue and pink dye into the stearin to colour it violet and stir. Add the wax to the stearin and stir. To test the colour, drop a little wax onto some greaseproof paper and leave to dry.

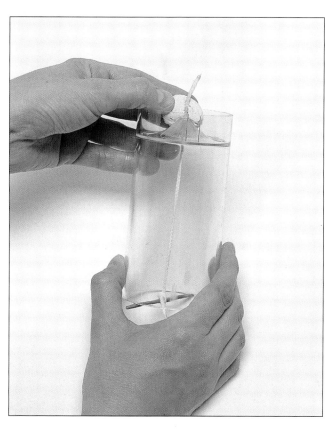

2 Remove the wax from the heat and allow it to cool while constantly stirring it with a fork, so that a skin does not appear on the top. A frothy scum will form on the surface as the wax cools.

3 Pour the frothy wax into the mould.

4 Immediately pour the wax back into the double boiler, leaving a coat of wax clinging to the inside of the mould.

5 Continue stirring the wax until it is frothy again then pour it slowly back into the mould. Keep the excess for topping up. After a few minutes, tap the side of the mould to release any air bubbles. Stand the mould in an empty water bath and place a weight on top. Fill the bowl with water to the level of the wax to cool it.

artist's tip

Create a set of frosted candles in cool, complementary shades. Colour the stearin with a little blue dye to create a cool aqua candle, or mix small amounts of blue and yellow dye to produce a minty green candle.

6 Leave to cool for 1 hour. By this time a well will have formed around the wick. Prick the wax around the wick with a needle. Reheat the wax and let it cool to 65°C (150°F). Use this to top up the well to just below the previously poured level. Leave to cool completely in the bowl of water, then remove the mould seal and slip the candle out of the mould. Cut the wick level with the base of the candle and trim the wick at the top to 1.5 cm (⅝ in).

Templates

The templates on these pages are actual size. Either photocopy them straight from the page or trace round them and transfer to template paper.

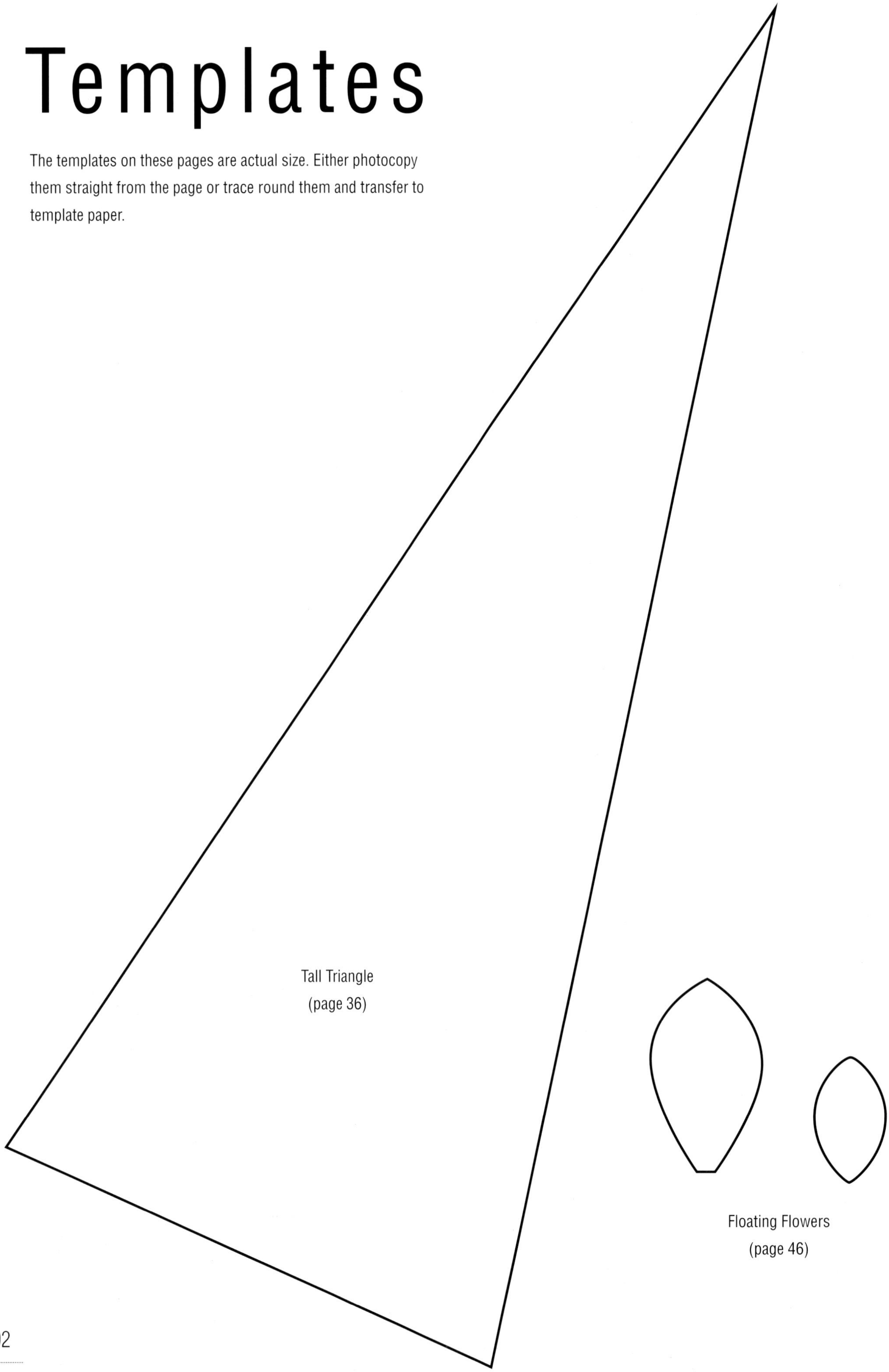

Tall Triangle
(page 36)

Floating Flowers
(page 46)

Oriental Candle motif

(page 54)

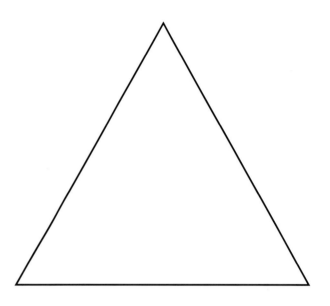

Stacked Triangles

(page 64)

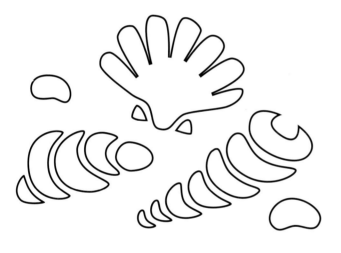

Shell Stencilled Lantern

(page 68)

Christmas Tree Candle

(page 74)

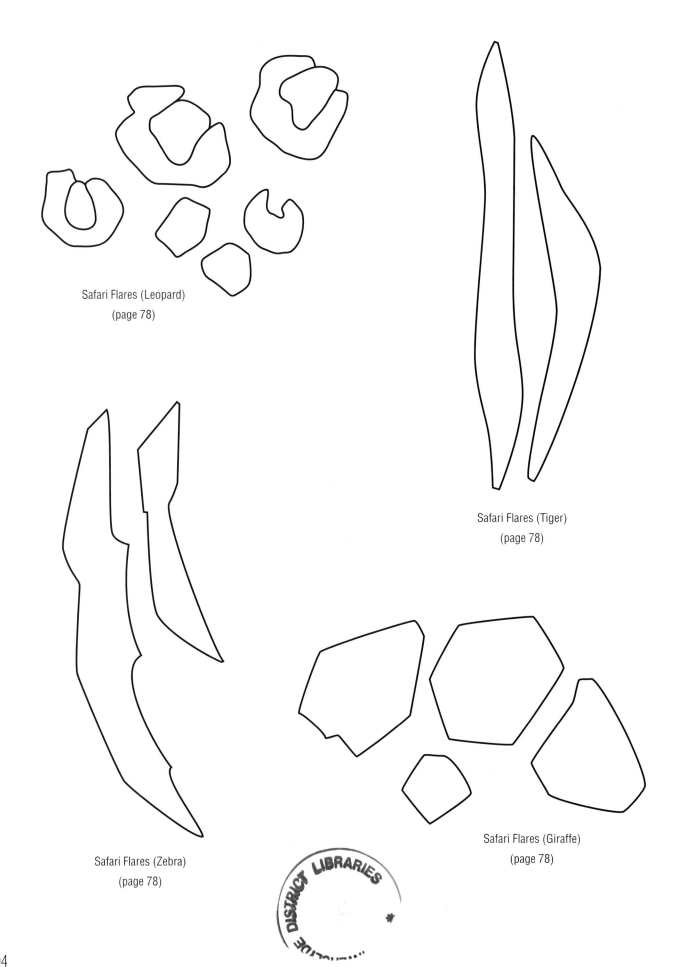

Safari Flares (Leopard)
(page 78)

Safari Flares (Tiger)
(page 78)

Safari Flares (Zebra)
(page 78)

Safari Flares (Giraffe)
(page 78)

Suppliers

UK

The Candle Shop
30 The Market
Covent Garden
London WC2E 8RE
Tel: 020 7379 4220
Fax: 020 7240 8065
Candle-making supplies

Candle Makers Supplies
28 Blythe Road
London W14 0HA
Tel: 020 7602 4031/2
Fax: 020 7602 2796
Shop and mail order candle-making supplies

Panduro Hobby
Westway House
Transport Avenue
Brentford
Middlesex TW8 9HF
Tel: 020 8847 6161
Fax: 020 8847 5073
Orders: 01392 427788
Mail order catalogue

E.H. Thorne Ltd
Beehive Works
Louth Road
Wragby
Lincolnshire LN3 5LA
Tel: 01673 858555
Fax: 01673 857004
Website: www.thorne.co.uk
Mail order beeswax and candle-making supplies

Homecrafts Direct
PO Box 38
Leicester LE1 9BU
Tel: 0116 251 3139
Mail order candle-making supplies

The Pier
200-203 Tottenham Court Road
London W1T 7PL
Tel: 020 7637 7001
Branches throughout the UK Candles and candle-holders

Senses Candle Design
5G Atlas Business Centre
Oxgate Lane
Staples Corner
London NW2 7HJ
Tel/Fax: 020 8450 3255
Candles and candle-making supplies

Websites:
www.waxworkshop.demon.co.uk
Candles, accessories, kits

www.wicksend.co.uk
Candles and candle-holders

SOUTH AFRICA

Crafty Suppliers
Shop 104
Upper Ground Level
The Atrium
Claremont,
Cape Town 7700
Tel: (021) 671 0286

Art, Craft & Hobbies
72 Hibernia Street
George, 6529
Tel/Fax: (0448) 74 1337

Artwise
337 Sanlam Centre
King's Road
Pinetown
Durban 3610
Tel: (031) 701 1824

Yours Forever Home
Craft Studio
92 Heritage Market
Hillcrest, 3610
Tel: (031) 765 6769

Southern Arts & Crafts
105 Main Street
Rosettenville
Johannesburg 2130
Tel/Fax: (011) 683 6566

AUSTRALIA

Arts and Craft Centre
34 Mint Street
East Victoria Park
WA 6101
Tel: (08) 9361 4567

Candle Creations
9 Francis Road
Wingfield
SA 5013
Tel: (08) 8347 2525

The Candle Factory
80 George Street
Sydney
NSW 2000
Tel: (02) 9241 3365

Candles Galore
11 Campbell Terrace
Alderley
Brisbane 4055
Tel: 1800 819 792

Gift Ware Agencies
Unit 207, West Point Centre
396 Scarborough Road
Osborne Park
WA 6017
Tel: (08) 9246 9445

Pacific Petroleum Products
1495 Warrego Highway
Ipswich
QLD 4305
Tel: (07) 3201 7566

Stacks of Wax
239 Australia Street
Newtown
NSW 2142
Tel: (02) 9660 0017

The Wizard of the Wick
Candle Co.
1/584 Waterworks Road
Ashgrove
QLD 4060
Tel: (07) 3366 7003
or write to
PO Box 2129
West Ashgrove 4060
Candle making classes

NEW ZEALAND

Aglow Wax & Wix
Box 7000
Auckland
Tel: (09) 834 6000

Golding Handcrafts
PO Box 9022
Wellington
Tel/Fax: (04) 801 5855
Website:
www.goldingcraft.com

Handcraft Supplies NZ Ltd
13-19 Rosebank Road
Avondale
Auckland
Tel: (09) 828 9834

National Candles Ltd
128 Egmont Street
PO Box 6024
Wellington
Tel: (04) 384 6806
Fax: (04) 384 7500

Waxglo House
1013 Ferry Road
Woolston
PO Box 19800
Christchurch
Tel: (03) 384 4188
Fax: (03) 384 4777

Index